Pop/Rock
Piano Favorit

Contents

Cover art by Levin Pfeufer

Transcribed by David Pearl

Cherry Lane Music Company
Director of Publications/Project Editor: Mark Phillips
Project Coordinator: Rebecca Skidmore

ISBN 978-1-60378-156-5

Africa

Words and Music by
David Paich and Jeff Porcaro

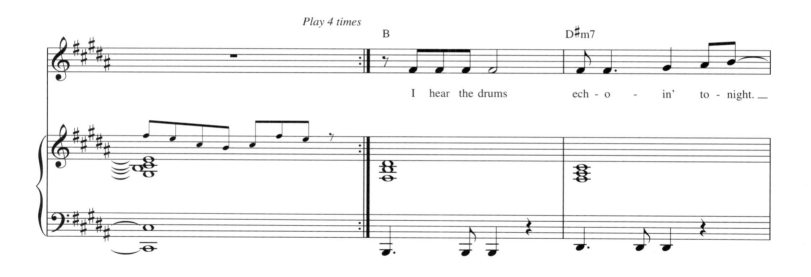

I hear the drums ech - o - in' to - night. __

__ She hears on - ly whis - pers of some

qui - et con - ver - sa - tion.

She's com - ing in, _____ twelve thir - ty flight. _____
The wild dogs cry _____ out in the night _____ as

Moon - lit wings _____ re - flect the stars _____ that guide me toward sal -
they grow rest - less, long - ing for _____ some sol - i - tar - y

va - tion.
com - pa - ny.

I stoppled an old ___ man a - long the way, ___ sure as
I know that I ___ must do what's right, ___ sure as

hop - ing to find ___ some old for - got - ten words ___ or an - cient
Kil - i - man - ja - ro ris - es like ___ O - lym - pus a - bove the

mel - o - dies.
Ser - en - get - i.

He turned to me ___ as if ___ to say, ___
I seek ___ to cure ___ what's deep ___ in - side, ___

F#m · D · A · E

I bless the rains __ down in Af - ri - ca. __

F#m · D · A

Gon - na take some time __ to do __ the things we nev - er

C#m · E · F#m · E/G#

had. __ Ooh,

A · G#m · C#m7

hoo.

6

"Hur - ry, boy, — she's wait-ing there — for you." —

Bennie and the Jets

Words and Music by
Elton John and Bernie Taupin

Intro

Slow, rigid tempo (♩ = 66)

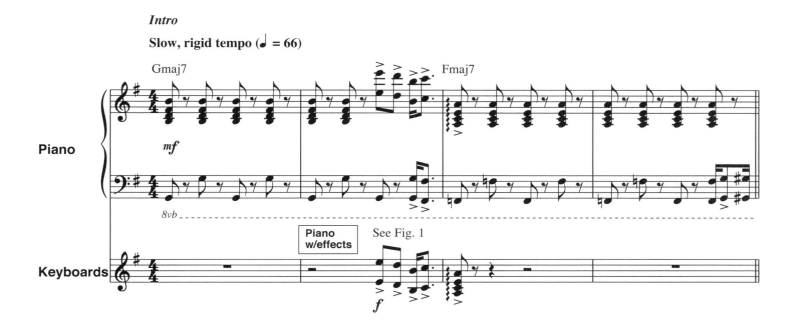

Verse

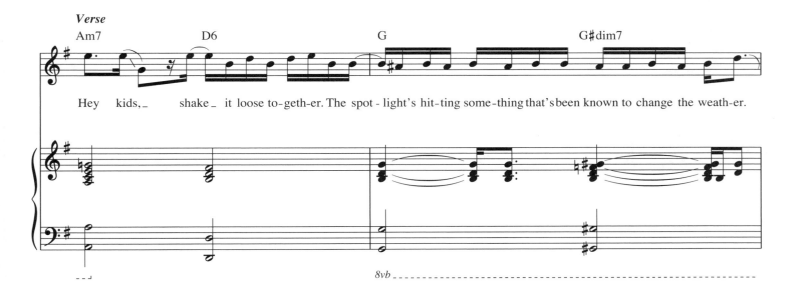

Hey kids,__ shake__ it loose to-geth-er. The spot - light's hit-ting some-thing that's been known to change the weath-er.

Fig. 1

- nie, she's a - real-ly keen. She's got e - lec-tric boots, a mo-hair suit. __ You know, I

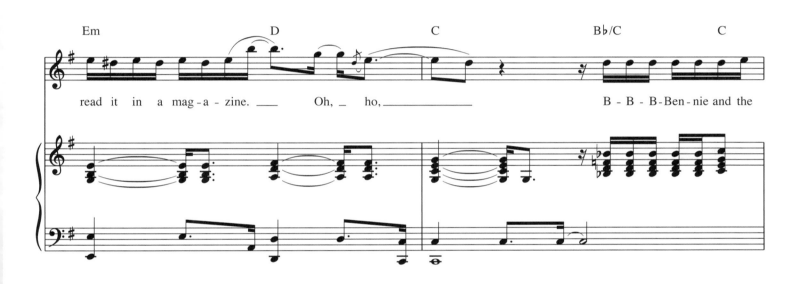

read it in a mag-a - zine. __ Oh, __ ho, _____ B - B - B-Ben - nie and the

Jets.

See Fig. 1

read it in a mag-a-zine. ___ Oh, _ ho, _____ B - B - B-Ben-nie and the

Jets.

Fill 2

15

Ben-nie, Ben-nie, Ben-nie, Ben - nie and the Jets._____

Ben - nie, Ben - nie, Ben - nie, Ben - nie, Ben - nie, Ben - nie, Ben -

nie, Ben-nie, Ben-nie, Ben-nie, Ben-nie and the Jets. __

Breathe
(2 AM)

Words and Music by
Anna Nalick

Moderately slow, in 2

Two A. M. and she calls ____ me 'cause I'm ____ still a - wake. ____ Can you help me un -
Two A. M. and I'm still ____ a - wake writ - ing a song. ____ If I get it all

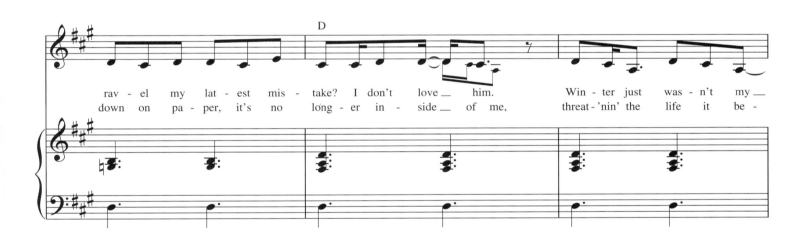

rav - el my lat - est mis - take? I don't love ____ him. Win - ter just was - n't my ____
down on pa - per, it's no long - er in - side ____ of me, threat - 'nin' the life it be -

____ sea - son. ____
longs to. ____
Yeah, we walk ____ through the doors, ____
And I feel ____ like I'm na -

so ac - cus - ing, their eyes, __ like they have an - y right at all to crit - i -
ked in front __ of the crowd, __ 'cause these words are my di - a - ry scream - in' a -

cize. Hyp - o - crites, you're all here for the ver - y same __ rea - son. __
loud. And I know that you'll use them how - ev - er you __ want to. __

'Cause
But } you can't __ jump the track. __ We're like cars on a ca - ble, and

life's like an ho - ur - glass glued to the ta - ble. No one can find __ the re - wind __

breathe. Woh, breathe, just

breathe. There's a light at each end of this

tun-nel. You shout 'cause you're just as far in as you'll ev-er be out. And these

mis-takes you've made, you'll just make them a-gain if you

Celebrate Me Home

Words by
Kenny Loggins

Music by
Kenny Loggins and Bob James

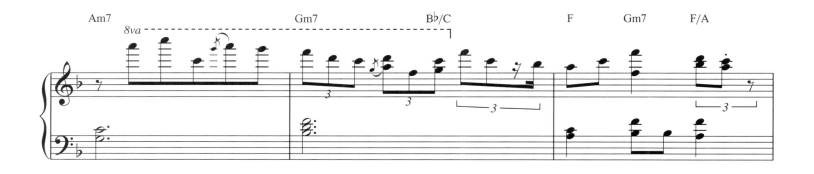

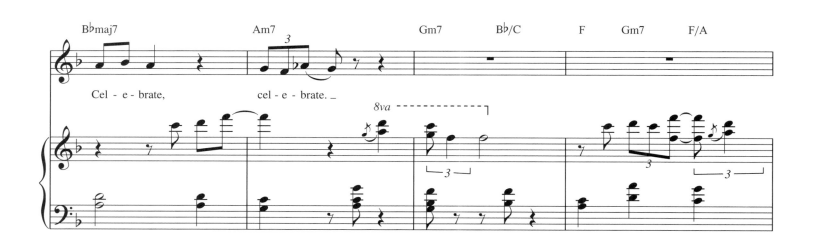

Cel - e - brate,   cel - e - brate. __

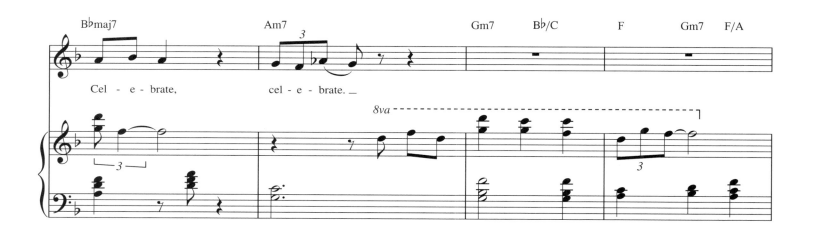

Cel - e - brate,   cel - e - brate. __

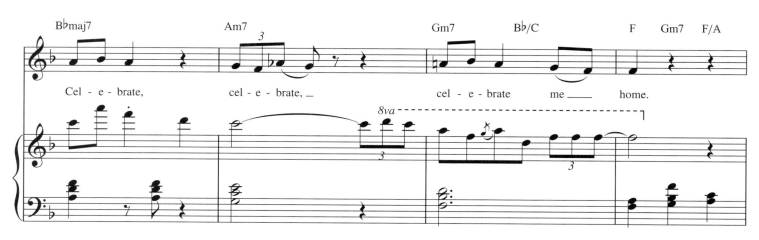

Cel - e - brate,   cel - e - brate, __   cel - e - brate   me ___ home.

Repeat and fade

36

Don't Stop Believin'

Words and Music by
Steve Perry, Neal Schon and Jonathan Cain

Just a   small - town   girl, ___
Just a   cit - y   boy, ___

liv - in' in a lone - ly world. _____

born and raised in south De - troit. _____

She took the mid - night train _____ go - in'

He took the mid - night train _____ go - in'

an - y - where. _____

an - y - where. _____

A sing-er in a smok-y room.

The smell of wine and cheap per-fume. ___ For a smile ___ they can

share the night. It goes on and on ___ and on ___ and on. ___

Stran - gers ___ wait - ing ___ up and down the
Street - light ___ peo - ple, ___ liv - ing just to

boul - e - vard, ___ their shad - ows ___ search - ing ___ in the night. ___
find e - mo - tion, hid - ing ___

some - where ___ in the night. ___

Work-in' hard ___ to get my fill. ___ Ev -'ry-bod - y wants a thrill. ___ Pay- in' an - y - thing to roll the dice ___ just

Coda

E   B   C#m7

A   E   B

G#m   A

E   B   C#m7

Don't __ stop   be - liev - in'.   Hold on to the

A   3   E   B   3

feel - in', _____ street - light   peo - ple. _____

43

Don't _ stop be -

liev - ing. Hold on, _____

street - light

peo - ple. _____

Repeat and fade

44

Gravity

Words and Music by
Sara Bareilles

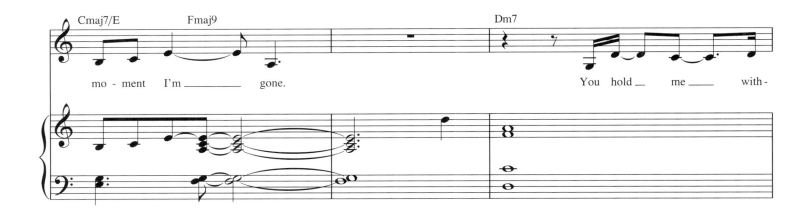

mo - ment I'm _____ gone. You hold __ me _____ with -

out touch. You keep __ me with - out _____ chains. ___

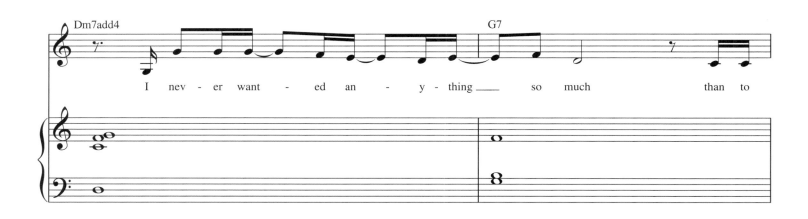

I nev - er want - ed an - y - thing ___ so much than to

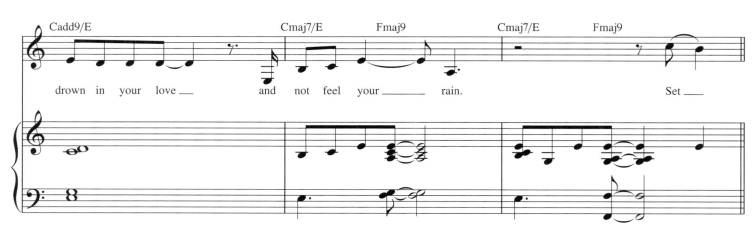

drown in your love ___ and not feel your _____ rain. Set ___

o - ver me.

I live here on ____ my knees __ as I try to make you see ___ that you're

ev - 'ry - thing I think __ I need _____ here on the ground. _____

But you're nei - ther friend __ nor foe, ___ though I can't ___ seem to let you go. ___

50

The one thing that I ___ still ___ know ___ is that you're keep - ing me down. ___

Woo. ___

You're keep - ing

me ___ down. _____

Hate to Lose Your Lovin'

Words and Music by
Paul Barrere and Craig Fuller

Moderately fast

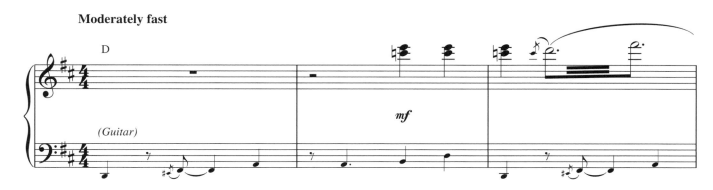

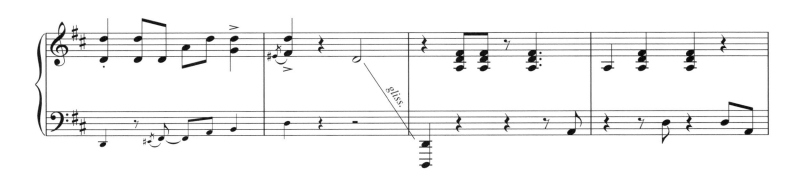

Last night I sat my ba-by right __ down and said, "The talk's all 'round the town. __ You're cheat-in' while I work all day. __ I guess that feel-in's __ fi-n'lly gone." __ And I got __ so tired __ of spend-ing my nights a-lone, __

and I packed ___ my bags ___ and I'm go-in' a-way. ___

But I sure would hate to lose ___ your lov-in', don't ya know. ___

If you said good-bye, it just would-n't seem right some - how. 'Cause it

felt so good, ___ whole lot bet-ter than I thought it

55

could. _____ Hon - ey, I'd hate to lose __ you now. __

Well, I swore __ I would - n't sit and cry __ 'cause my

ba - by left __ me both high and dry; would - n't sit and pine. __ Gon - na

57

lov-in', don't ya know. ___ If you said good-bye, it just

would-n't seem right some - how. 'Cause it felt so good, ___

whole lot bet - ter than I thought it could. ___

Hon - ey, I'd hate to lose ___ you now. ___

58

Well, I think it's gon - na be all right ___ 'cause I found ___ a lit - tle

girl last night. And she said, "Ya bet - ter just move on in ___

'cause I got my rent paid through next week ___ and I'll be

out to - night." ___ But don't you know that I'll

do my best __ to be back by ten __ and I sure would __

hate to lose __ your lov-in', don't ya know. __ If you

said good-bye, it just wouldn't seem right some-how. 'Cause it felt so good, __

__ whole lot bet-ter than I thought it could. _____

Hon - ey, I'd hate to lose ___ you now. ___   Don't ya know,

hon - ey, I'd hate to lose ___ you now. ___   Tryin' - a tell ya,

hon - ey, I'd hate to lose ___ you now. ___

Home Sweet Home

Words and Music by
Tommy Lee and Nikki Sixx

song and you'll nev-er be __ left all a-lone. __ Take me to your heart; feel me in your

bones. Just one more night and I'm com-ing off __ this long and wind - ing road. __

I'm on my way, __ I'm on my way; _____ home sweet

home. To - night, to - night, ___ { I'm on my way, __ I'm on my
                                    { I'm on my way. ___ Just set me

free; ____ home ____ sweet ____ home. _____

Hmm, _____ hmm, _____ hmm, ___

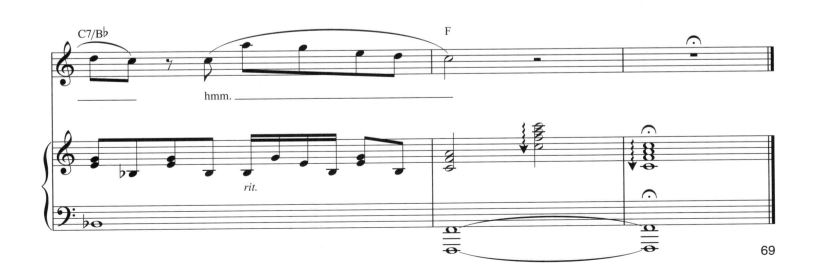

_____ hmm. _____

I Can't Make You Love Me

Words and Music by
Mike Reid and Allen Shamblin

*Chord symbols reflect basic harmony.

Turn down the ___ lights, ___ turn down ___ the bed, ___

make you love me if you don't. You can't make your heart feel

some-thing it won't. Here in the dark in

these fi - nal ho - urs, I will lay down my heart and

I'll feel the pow - er. But you won't, no, you won't. 'Cause I can't

It Don't Have to Change

Words and Music by
John Stephens and Dave Tozer

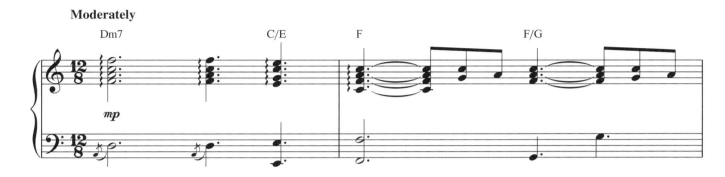

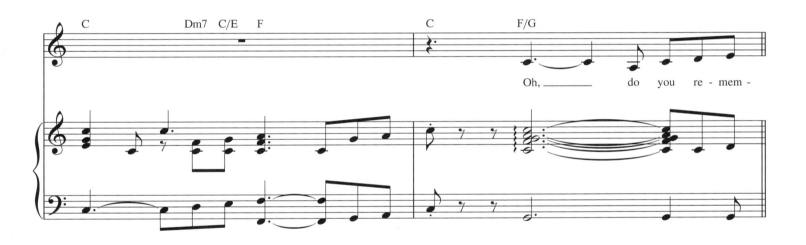

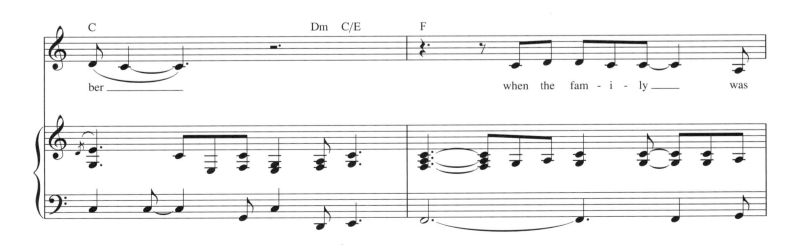

ev - 'ry - thing? ___   Oh, _____ do you re - mem -

ber? _____   It was so long ___ a - go ___ and

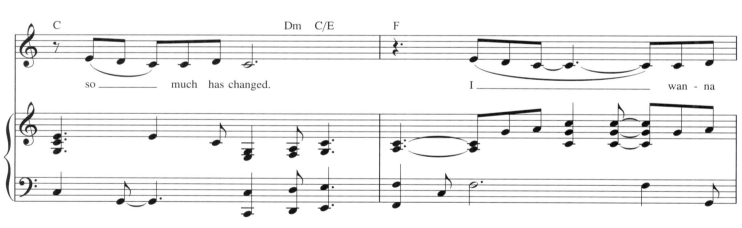

so ___ much has changed.   I _____ wan - na

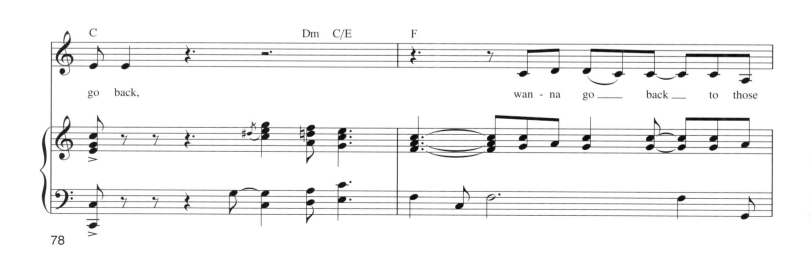

go back,   wan - na go ___ back ___ to those

The Long and Winding Road

Words and Music by
John Lennon and Paul McCartney

It al-ways leads _ me here, leads me to your door.

Verse %

(1.) The wild and wind-y night _ that the rain _ washed a-way _
(2., D.S.) still they lead me back _ to the long _ wind-ing road. _

Fm   Bb7   Eb   **1. Bridge** Eb/Bb   Ab

Let me know   the   way. _____
Lead me to _____ your door. _____

Man-y times_I've been a-lone   and

Eb/G   Fm   Bb7   Eb/Bb   Ab   Eb/G   Fm   Bb7

man-y times_ I've cried. _   An-y-way   you'll nev-er know   the   man-y times_I've tried. _   And

But

CODA

Lead me to your ___ door. _____ Yeah yeah yeah yeah. _

Look What You've Done to Me

Words and Music by
Boz Scaggs and David Foster

90

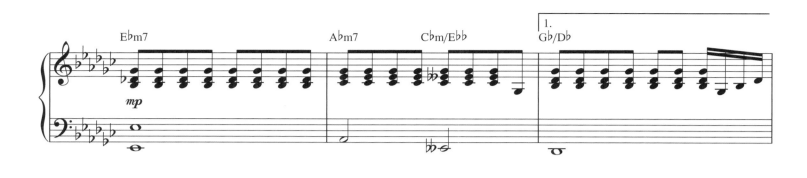

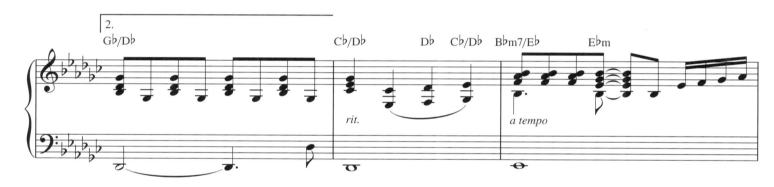

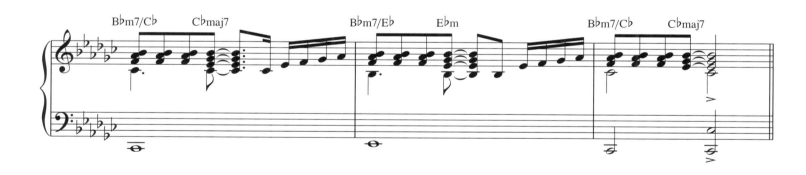

Love, _____ look what you've done to me. __

Mandolin Rain

Words and Music by
B.R. Hornsby and John Hornsby

man - do - lin rain. _____ Lis - ten to the mu - sic on the lake. Oh, lis - ten to my

heart break _____ ev - 'ry time she runs _ a - way. _____ Oh, lis - ten to the

ban - jo wind, _____ a sad song drift - ing low. Lis - ten to the

tears roll _____ down my face as she turns to go. _____

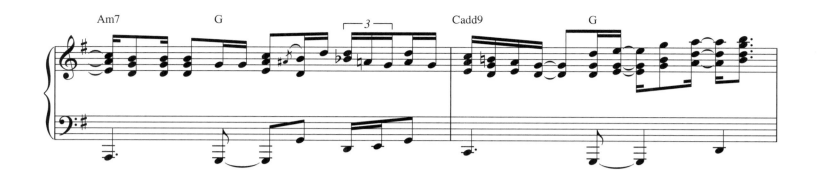

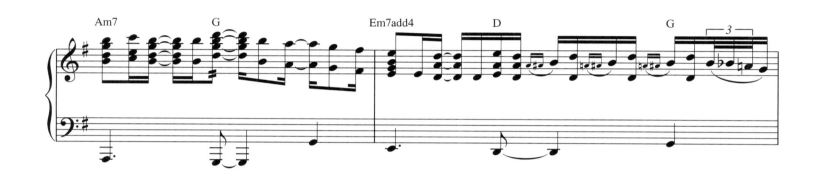

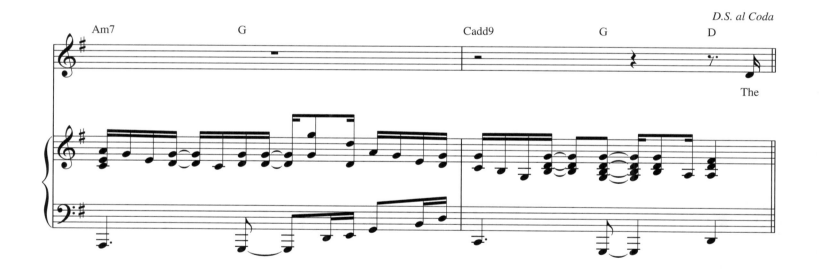

long a - go. ___ Lis - ten to the man - do - lin rain. ___ Lis - ten to the

turns to go. Lis - ten to the tears _____ roll down my face as she

turns to go. _____

w/ vocal ad lib till end

Begin fade

Fade out

New York State of Mind

Words and Music by
Billy Joel

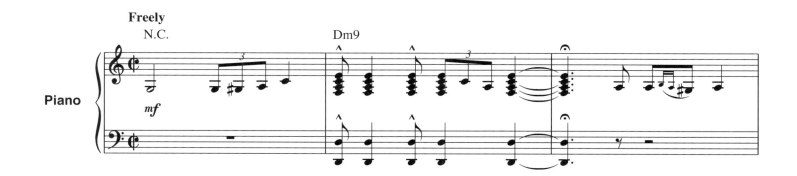

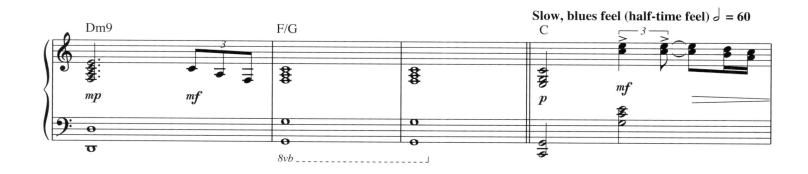

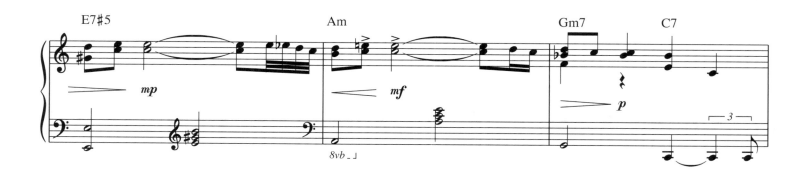

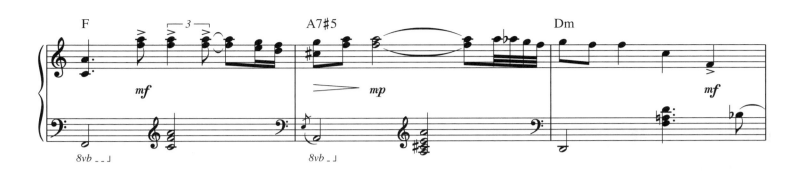

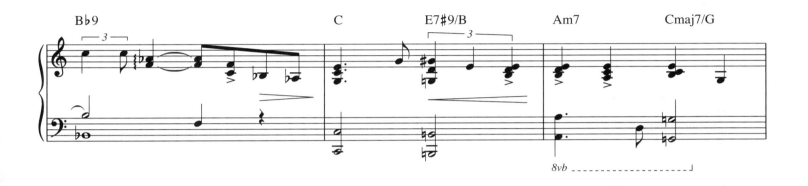

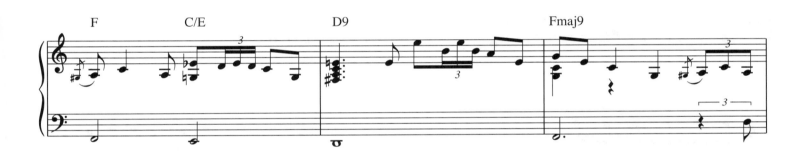

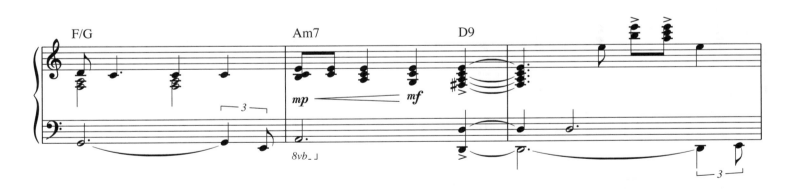

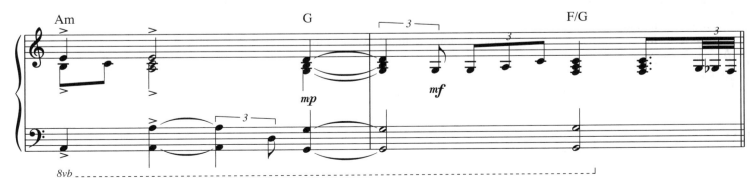

with the rhy - thm and ____ blues. _____

Well, now I ____ need ____ a ____ lit - tle give and take, ____

____ the New York Times, _____ the

Dai - ly News. _____

Play Fill 4 (2nd time)

It comes down to re-al-i-ty and it's fine with me 'cause I've let it slide I don't care if it's Chi-na-town or on Riv-er-side. I don't have an-y rea-sons. I've left them all be-hind.

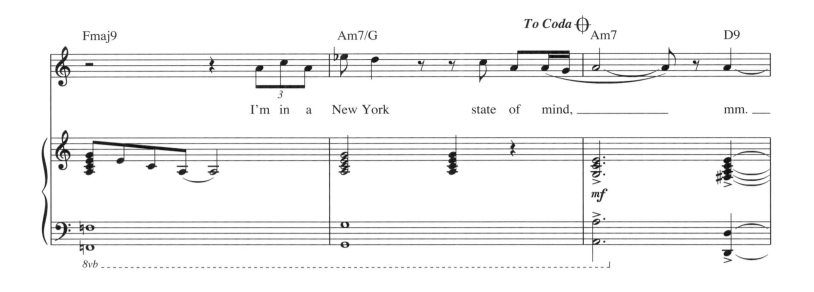

I'm in a   New York   state of   mind, _____   mm. _____

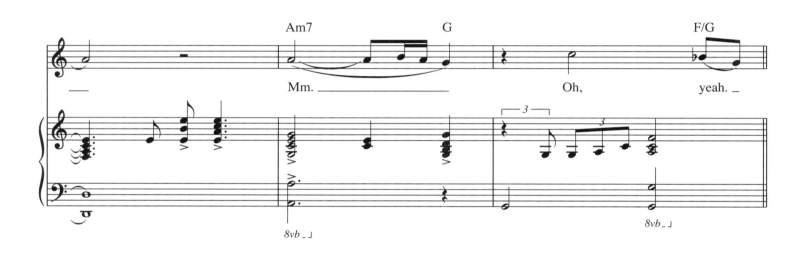

Mm. _____   Oh,   yeah. _

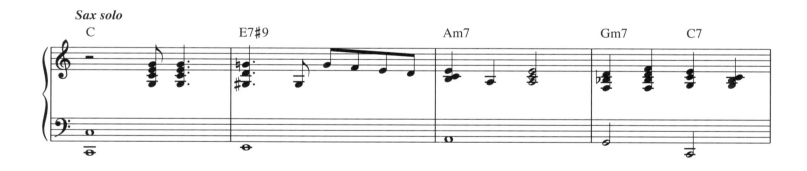

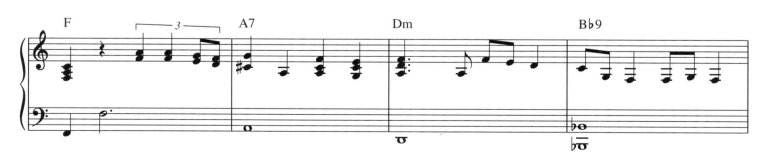

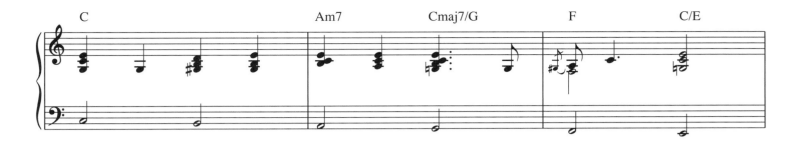

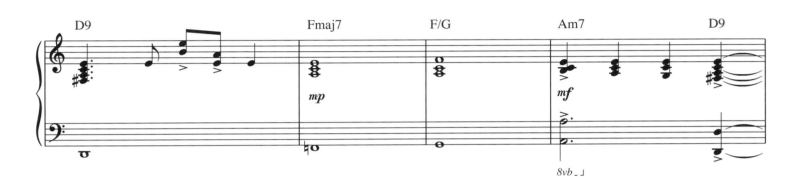

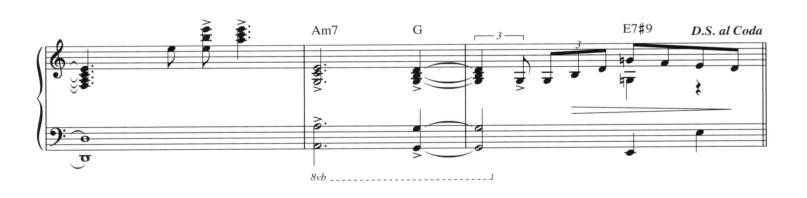

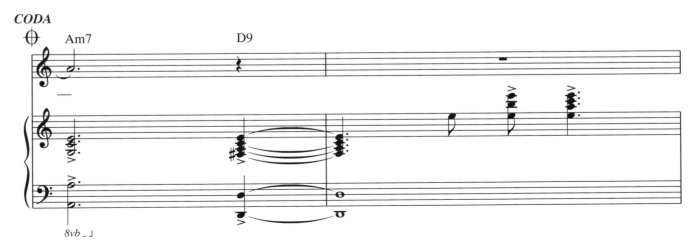

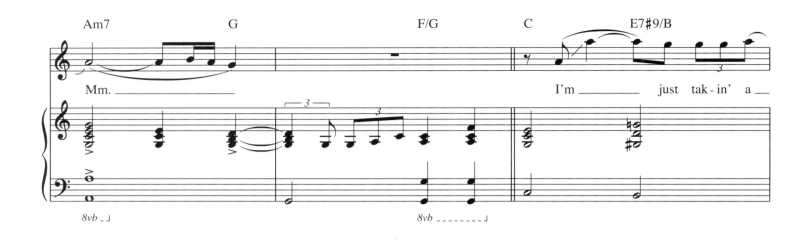

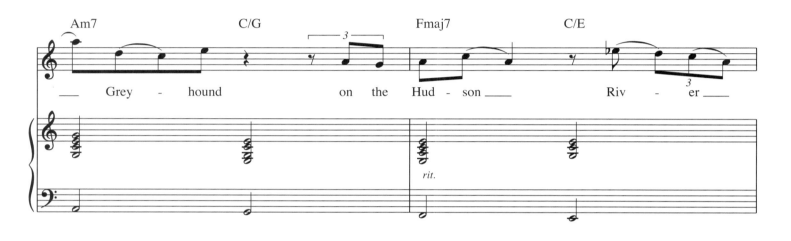

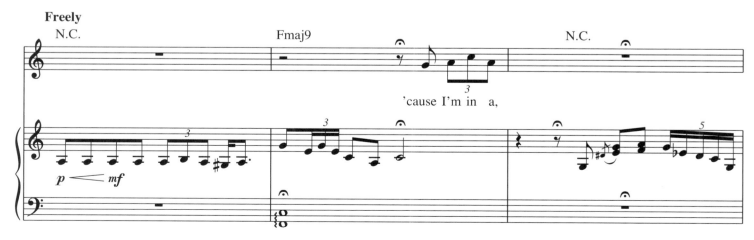

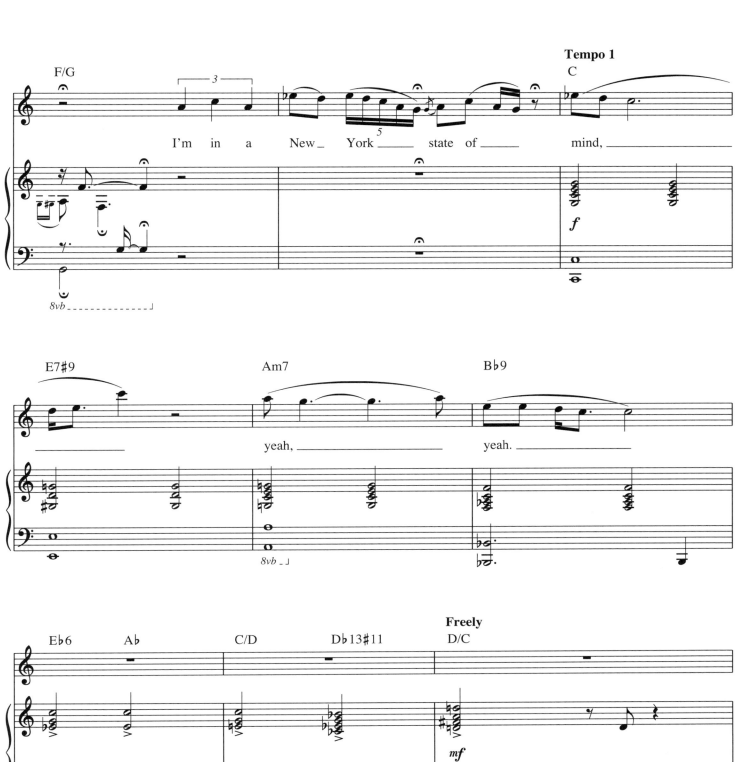

I'm in a New York state of mind, yeah, yeah.

Rosanna

Words and Music by
David Paich

All I wan-na do when I wake up in the morn-ing is

I can see your face still shin-ing through the win-dow on the

see your eyes, _____ Ro - san - na, ___ Ro - san - na.

oth - er side, _____ Ro - san - na, ___ Ro - san - na.

I did-n't know you were look-in' for more ___ than I ___ could ev - er be.
I nev - er thought that ___ los - in' ___ you ___ could ev - er hurt so bad. ___

1.2.3. Not quite a year ___ since you

went a - way, ___ Ro - san - na, ___ yeah.

Now she's gone and I

114

Still Crazy After All These Years

Words and Music by
Paul Simon

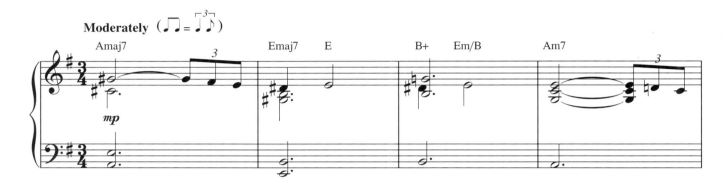

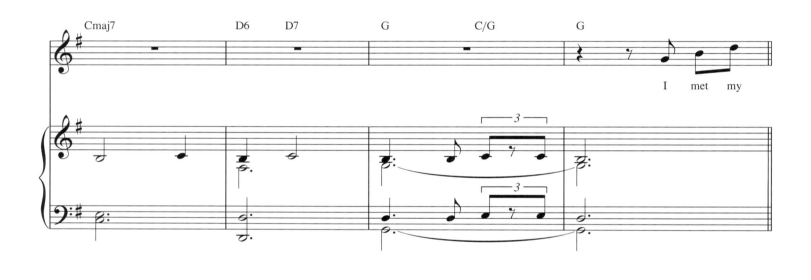

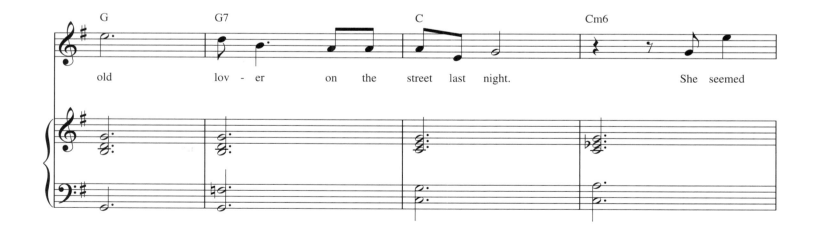

Now I sit by my win-dow ___ ___ and I watch ___ the cars. ___ I fear ___ I'll do ___ some dam-age one fine ___ day. ___

We Belong Together

Words and Music by
Rickie Lee Jones

Moderately slow, in 4

1. I say this was

no game of chick-en; you were aim-ing your best friend   that you wear like a

2.3. See additional lyrics

switch-blade on a chain a-round your neck. I think you picked this up in Mex-i-co from your dad. Now it's

D/G

Dad-dy on the booze and it's Bran-do on the ice. Now it's

D   *To Coda* ⊕

Dean in the door-way with one more way he can't play _____ this scene _____ twice. So you

Bm/F#

drug her down ev-'ry drag of this for-bid-den fit of love and you told her to stand tall when you kissed her. But that's

geth - er.

Additional Lyrics

2. Once Johnny the King made a spit ring,
  And all the skid kids saw a very, very proud man.
  And he entwine her in his finger
  And she lay there like a baby in his hand
  And climb upon the rooftop docks
  Lookin' out on the crosstown seas.
  And he wraps his jacket across her shoulders
  And he falls and hugs and holds her on his knees.
  But a sailor just takes a broad
  Down to the dark end of the fair
  To turn her into a tattoo that will whisper
  Into the back of Johnny's black hair.
  And now Johnny the King walks these streets
  Without her in the rain
  Lookin' for a leather jacket
  And a girl who wrote her name forever.
  A promise that
  We belong together,
  We belong together.

3. Shall we weigh along these streets
  Young lions on the lam?
  Are the signs you hid deep in your heart
  All left on neon for them?
  Who are foolish?
  Who are victim
  Of the sailors and the ducky boys
  Who would move into your eyes and lips
  And every tear that falls down on the neighborhood now. *(To Coda)*

When You Love a Woman

Words by
Steve Perry and Jonathan Cain

Music by
Steve Perry, Jonathan Cain and Neal Schon

In my life __ I see where I've been. __
If I can't be - lieve __ that some - one is true, __

I said that I'd nev - er fall a - gain. __
to fall in love is so hard to do. __

132

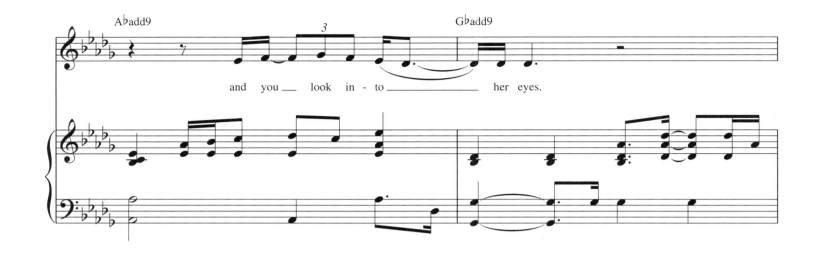

and you look in-to her eyes.

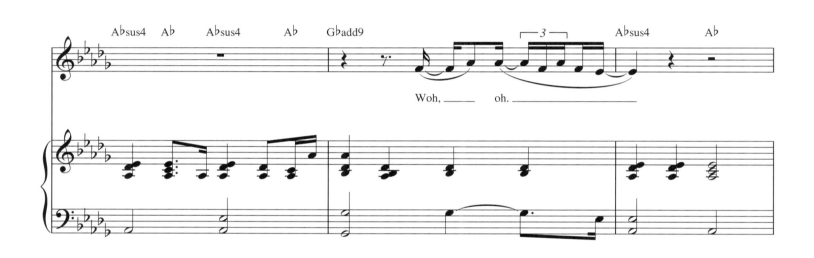

Woh, oh.

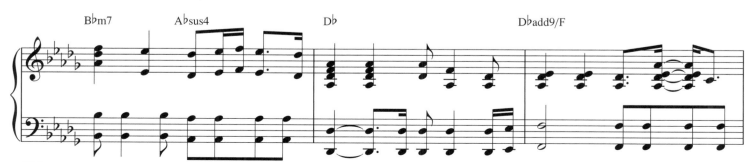

Yesterdays

Words and Music by
W. Axl Rose, West Arkeen,
Billy McCloud and Del James

Moderately slow

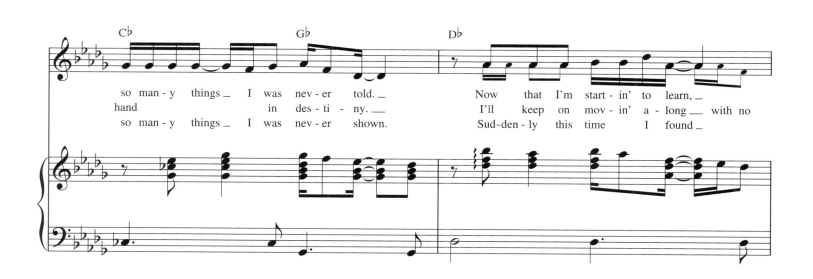

got noth - in' for me.

Got noth - in' for me.

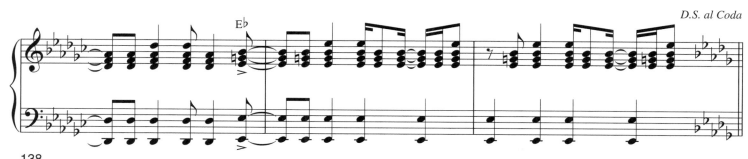

D.S. al Coda